Duets with a Difference

Piano Time Duets Book 1

new edition

Pauline Hall

MUSIC DEPARTMENT

OXFORD
UNIVERSITY PRESS

Great Clarendon Street, Oxford OX2 6DP, England
198 Madison Avenue, New York, NY10016, USA

First published 1989
New edition 2005

25

ISBN 978–0–19–372753–3

Music and text origination by
Barnes Music Engraving Ltd., East Sussex
Printed in Great Britain on acid-free paper by
Halstan & Co. Ltd., Amersham, Bucks.

Copyright acknowledgements

Contents

Except in Royal procession the pupil plays Primo, but you might also like to try the easier Secondos.

Stepping out!

Alan Bullard

Lively

Emerald Isle

Pauline Hall

Gently

In these two pieces your hands stay over the same notes throughout.

Stepping out!

Lively

Alan Bullard

both hands an octave higher throughout

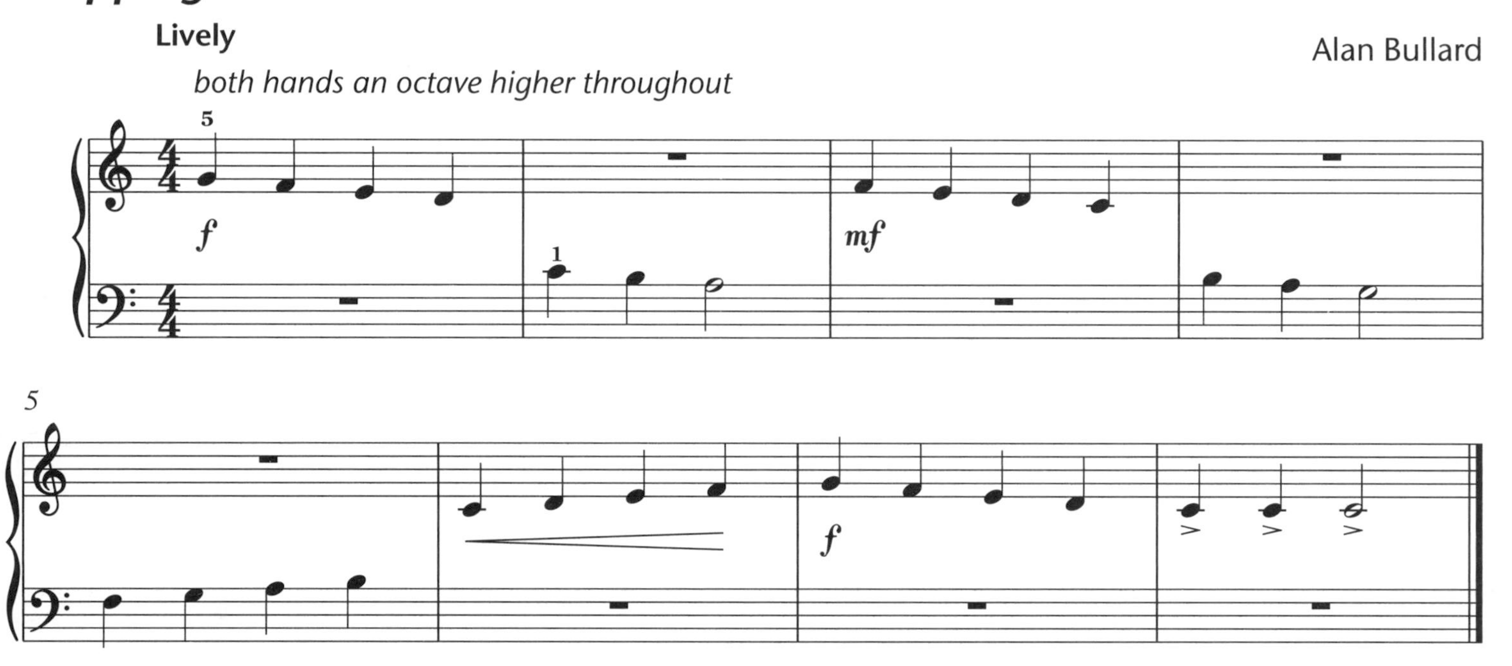

Emerald Isle

Gently

Pauline Hall

both hands an octave higher throughout

The Irish washerwoman

arr. Pauline Hall

The Irish washerwoman

This jolly Irish jig needs to swing along at a good, brisk pace—but don't let it hurry. It will need slow practice at first to get it neat.

Andante cantabile

Anton Diabelli (1781–1858)
Op. 149 No. 2

Andante cantabile

In this piece your right hand only plays an octave higher. Both hands use the treble clef.

Anton Diabelli (1781–1858)
Op. 149 No. 2

Lullaby

Harold Scull

Lullaby

Play this very smoothly and gently. Your hands stay over these 5 notes:
Your right hand plays an octave higher.

Harold Scull

Black key lullaby

Make up a lullaby duet of your own, using only the black keys.

Here are the words and rhythm for your lullaby. Read the words in time, and see how they fit to the notes:

Moonlight is gleaming
Silver and bright.
Sleep, baby softly,
Soon dawn will break.
When the bright sunshine
Tells you to wake.

Now make up a tune, using the following tips to help you:

- Start and finish your melody on F sharp. Remember, use only the black keys!

Start and finish here.

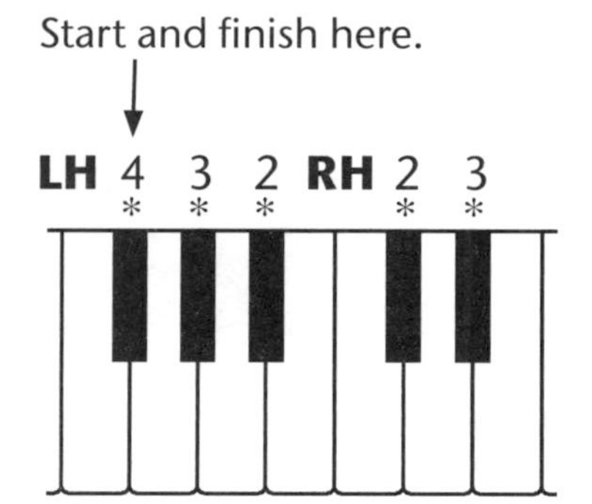

- Don't let your tune jump about—keep it on nearby notes.
- Let your tune fit the words by thinking the words as you make up your tune.

Secondo Play an accompaniment using F sharp major, or make up your own accompaniment using suitable chords.

Now play the lullaby together.

Royal procession

For this piece you need to swap seats. Primo uses both hands, while Secondo (pupil) plays four notes only:

The duet parts are written one below the other.

Pauline Hall

Donkey ride

Elsie Wells

Donkey ride

Elsie Wells

Allegro

Jurriaan Andriessen

Allegro

Your hands stay over these notes:

Jurriaan Andriessen

L·I·S·T·E·N·I·N·G G·A·M·E·S

Guess what?

Player 2 (or teacher) Play the five notes from middle C to the G above:

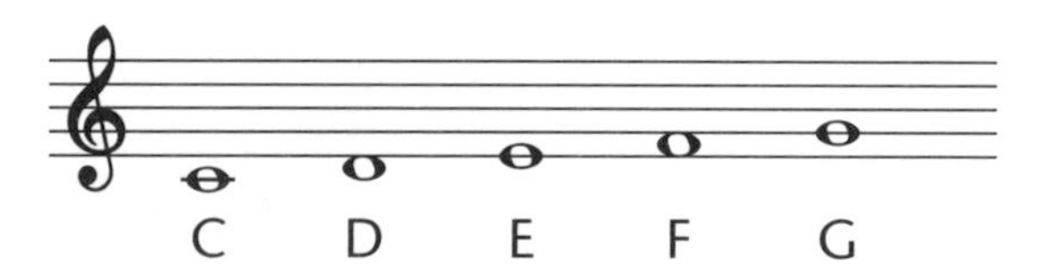

Player 1 Shut eyes (don't cheat!).
Player 2 Play middle C, then another note between D and G.
Player 1 Name the note, then play it.

When you can get five right in a row, try the game from other starting notes. Can you still get five in a row?

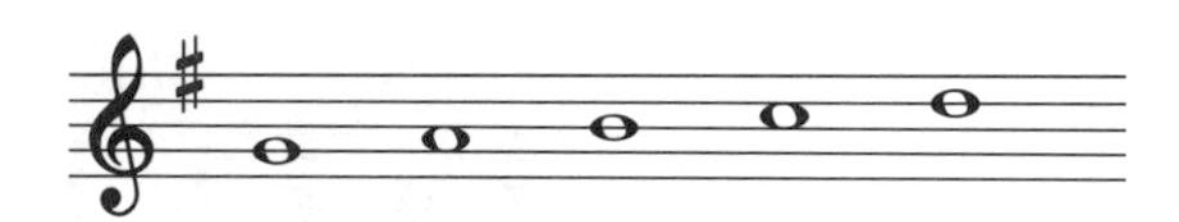

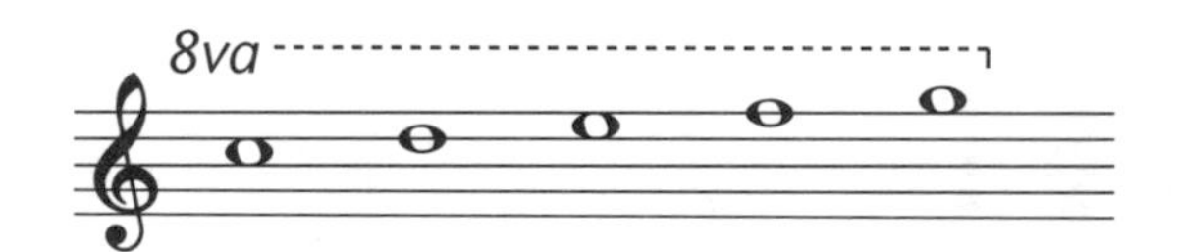

Player 2 Now play middle C and then another note between D and G—but there's no need for Player 1 to shut their eyes. Instead of naming the note, can you think of a song that begins with these notes?

For example:

'Baa, baa black sheep'

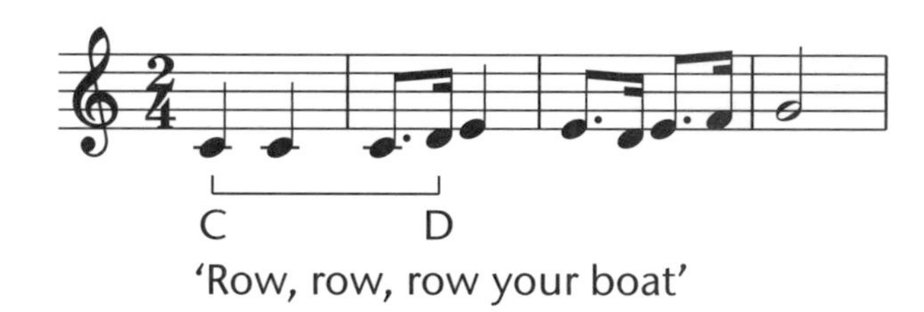

'Row, row, row your boat'

Take two

Player 2 (or teacher) Play two notes together—choose notes that are not more than an octave apart.
Player 1 Sing or hum the top note.
Player 2 Play the two notes again.
Player 1 Sing or hum the lower note.

Can you get five right in a row?

Copy cat

For this game, you should use only the notes of the G major scale.

Player 1 Play the G above middle C and add one more note of your choice. The new note must be next door or one away.
Player 2 Play these two notes and add another one, like this:

Player 1 Play these notes and then a fourth one. And so on.

The game goes on until someone forgets!

Spot the difference

This game is just like a traditional 'spot the difference', but with music. How good a listener are you?

Player 2 (teacher) Play the following extract:
Player 1 Listen carefully.

Player 2 Play the extract again, but this time change one of the following features—don't say which one!

- Play *forte*
- Play staccato
- Play in D major
- Play crotchets instead of dotted minims
- Play crotchets instead of dotted crotchets
- Don't use the pedal

Player 1 Can you spot what has changed?

The whole of this piece is in *Piano Time Pieces* book 2. Try this game with other pieces.

The Derry boat

The duet parts are written one below the other—make sure you can follow your part before you play. Can you hear the rolling waves?

trad.
arr. Alan Bullard

13
mf
mf
17
p
p
21
rit.
pp
rit.
pp

March

Karl Wohlfahrt (1874–1943)

Andante

March

Your hands stay over these notes:

Karl Wohlfahrt (1874–1943)

Andante

Swinging fingers

Alan Bullard

Blues for two

Try improvising a blues duet.

Player 2 (teacher) Play left hand throughout and right hand in odd-numbered bars. In the right hand play just the note C, but use a variety of one-bar rhythms—we've given a start. Add in some rests!

Player 1 Play right hand in even-numbered bars, echoing Player 2's rhythm one octave higher.

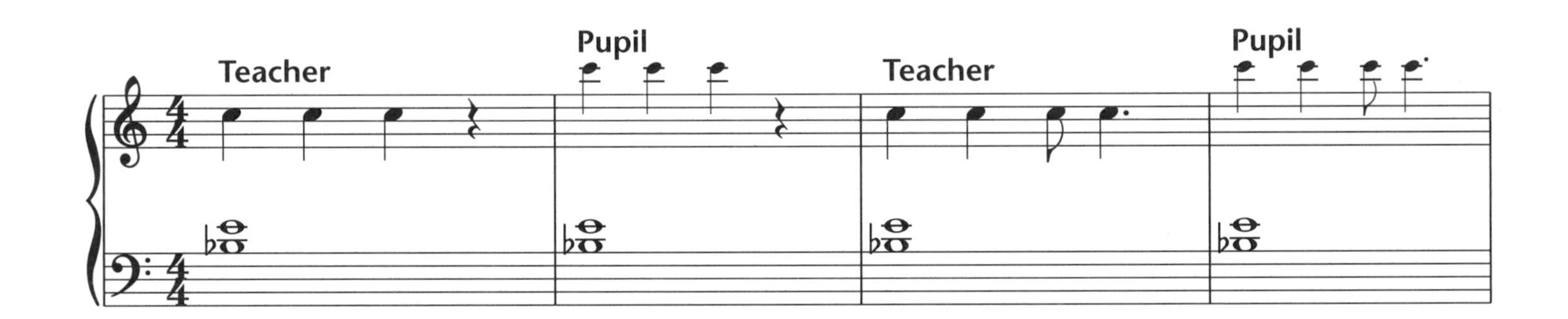

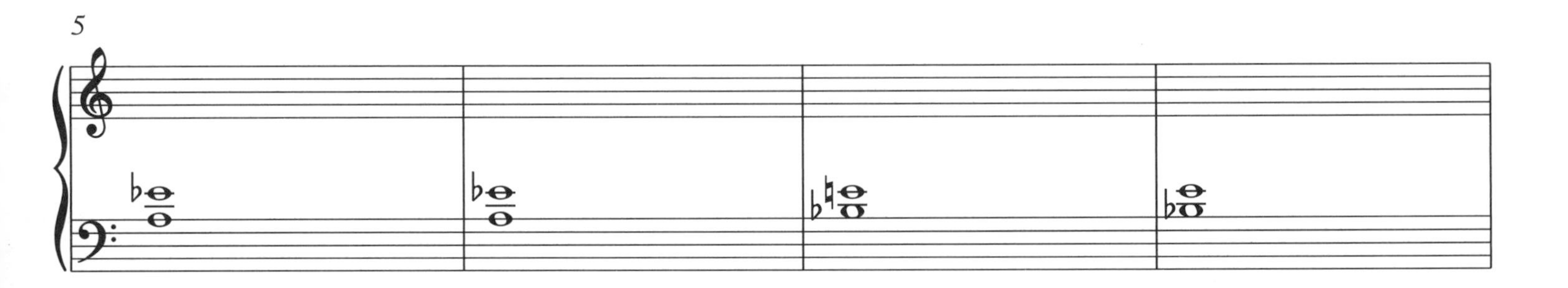

9

repeat ad lib.

last time

This could be extended by varying the pitches: the notes C, A, and G work well.

Berceuse

Adam Carse (1878–1958)

Berceuse

Andantino
Adam Carse (1878–1958)
8va
pp
mf
cresc.
dim.
poco rall.
a tempo
rall.

Camptown races

arr. Pauline Hall

16
mp
21
f
26
mf
p
ff
ff

Moderato

Anton Diabelli (1781–1858)
Op. 149 No. 3
Moderato
8va
Primo
Moderato
Secondo
p
f

21
8va
fz
p
mf
27
8va
f
33
8va
p
p
p

39
8va
cresc.
cresc.
45
8va
f
p
f
p
51
8va
f
f